GRATITUDE
Two Hundred Short Poems

A.H. MORRIS

Gratitude: Two Hundred Short Poems
Published by BluePen Publishing
New Canaan, CT

Copyright ©2024 by A.H. Morris. All rights reserved.

No part of this book may be reproduced in any form or by any mechanical means, including information storage and retrieval systems without permission in writing from the publisher/author, except by a reviewer who may quote passages in a review.

All images, logos, quotes, and trademarks included in this book are subject to use according to trademark and copyright laws of the United States of America.

Inquiries can contact: ahmorris200@gmail.com

ISBN: 979-8-218-24568-9

POETRY / General

Cover and interior design by Asya Blue Design, copyright owned by A.H. Morris.
Illustrated cover art by A.H. Morris.

All rights reserved by A.H. Morris and BluePen Publishing.

Printed in the United States of America.

Dedication:

To those who practice kindness,
compassion, and love

Acknowledgments:

Ron and Susan Scolastico for inspiration
Jeannie Lawson for encouragement
Debbie Bancroft for friendship
Amanda Miller for the finish line
My wife, Melissa, for love, always

1

Art:
Take the ordinary
And invite spirits
To participate.

2
―

Feeling/reason:
Two truths
That wrestle.
Consider love:
Impossible
Paradox,
Transcendent.

3

I can't recall
What mind I had
When I was young,
As I will soon
Forget the one
Believing this.

4

I will stop talking
And make my feet smile.
Then bring it back up
Through body to head
And hope it will stay.

5

We live from present
Into the past while
The future wonders
What were we thinking.

6

Tonight I am the
Acrobat halfway
Across emptiness
Knowing the landing
Is too far away.

7

I dread sunrise.
Bad choices accumulated,
Sensible sleep abandoned,
Too late, this moment
Of bearing witness
In defeated silence
To a weakening sky's
First orange wisps.
Chaos exhausted,
All reason is lost.

8

Tell me a joke
So we may share
Our defiance
Of hopelessness.

9

I am a miner
Panning the details
Of our days to find
That nugget of truth
To perfectly show
Who you are to me.

10

Choices,
Constant.
Step up,
Step down.
Right/wrong.
Is there
A big
Picture?

11
———

I must find
My coat of
Acceptance
Before I
Go to meet
Winter's freeze.

Three o'clock:
Best described
As non-descript.
Afternoon's midriff,
Not a meal in sight.
It sags, unloved,
Sitting patiently
On the tarmac
Of cocktail's runway.

13

You and I -
Earth and moon,
Coupled in
The unknown,
Maintaining
Attraction,
As it was
Meant to be.

14

The future,
Secure or
Chaotic,
Has our fates
Intertwined.

15

Complications
I don't deserve.
Happiness must
Wait until I'm
Done with worry.

The garden boasts its fullness -
Fresh green with yellows and whites.
Welcoming, and carefree
Of its imminent demise.

17

On terry cloth,
Oceanside chaise,
Under the sun.
The children play
With buckets
By the sea.
Newspapers
From the north,
Reporting snow.
I toss them
To the sand,
Lean back,
And think of
Lunch.

18

A ride through the tunnel
Where the shadows are real
And what we know scatters.
We emerge from terrors
With so much to say yet
No one waiting to hear.

19

Tonight will be unlike
Any that came before.
I have found my courage,
Vast blackness has been tamed.
I will reach heavenward
Into constellations,
And touch magnificence.

20
———

How do I separate
How I see you from so
Many years together?
We have transformed but the
First spark, the origin
Of us, remains always.

21

My car, my body
In need of repairs.
I am comforted
By the familiar,
But overcome by
The worry of the
Breakdown that will leave
Me lost and alone,
No way to get home.

22

It was significant,
And I needed your help.
Either through negligence
Or perhaps cruelty,
You chose to ignore it.
What is left for me now
Is to love you again.

I step into the now
To see what I can see.
I find beauty and pain,
But did not expect how
Quiet it is, and filled
With possibilities.

He was a sweet boy.
He made us laugh.
My resolve cracked
And I have fallen on
The rocks of grief.
I have lost my lifelines
Of intellect, guile and ego.
I am lost in the land
Of sadness knowing
I must find a reason
Before I can return.
I will be here a while.

25
―――

Our property
Reawakens,
Fills with color.
And yet the joy
Is unfulfilled,
Diminished by
What is missing:
Half of my heart.

I have walked miles on
A trying path to
This pond at sunset.
Two deer arrive and
Looking up, see me,
But stay, not afraid.
They understand more
Than I ever will.

27
———

To feel God,
I close my eyes.
To see God,
I open them.

This morning
All pieces
Are in place.
We begin
Our path
To find
New altitudes
Of happiness.

29

We are based on a
Gallant promise from
Two decades ago.
We have kept our word.
Is it good fortune
Or could we have known
The unknowable?

30

Time takes from my body.
People take from my strength
Until I am hollow.
It's then I determine
I have always been whole.

31

Angels break their silence
In ways just short of proof.
We feel their soft presence.
Was it them? Maybe so.

I sleep
In the basement
Among the past,
Isolated
From reason.

33

Poison
Of my dreams:
Ghouls,
Dance complete,
Don't leave,
But quietly
Return home.

34

The years have
Reduced me.
Pared and patched
Always change.
Left with less,
Now I am
More thankful.

35

I stumble,
Second guess,
Rethink
Fall short
Feel guilty;
All perfect
Imperfection.

Our egos spar,
Fearing demise.
Hearts look on,
Mortified.

37

I ponder:
Spontaneity
Or anticipation.
Which is more
Delightful?

We are mired
As adversaries
Through an
Endless night,
Stomping
Our structure
Of sacrifice,
Leaving
Too little
To salvage.

Soft summer night
Under the stars.
A private jet
Now interrupts.
I envision
A businessman
Reading papers,
Unaware he's
Passing through
God's Heaven.

40

I am a rowboat
Loose from its mooring
Adrift on the lake.
I will wash ashore
In some wooded cove
Having found a home.

War monuments
Are carved from stone
For permanence,
The opposite
Of bravery.

42

Lies:
The mind will
Justify,
But the heart
Knows better.

Late afternoon
Summer storm
Fills the streets,
Cursed by pedestrians,
Inspiration to the poet.

The grace of
Nightmares is
They defy
Possession.

The sweetest
Note contains
As one, both
Happiness
And sorrow.

The spotlight moon
Crisscrosses
Sentinel trees
With dark light
On silver snow.
Far from home,
I am here to
Celebrate the
Magnificence
Of solitude.

Happiness
Is earned,
Not by the
Avoidance,
But with the
Approval
Of Sadness.

Dawn's light across
Summer's valley as
Life reawakens.
We have talked
Through the night,
Defying sleep,
Unresolved.
Quiet returns.
This day begins in
Beauty and sadness.

49

Wisdom
Surrounds me
But it speaks
A foreign
Language.

50

I wonder why I am
The only person who
At this moment believes
This is the place to be.

51

Thorns on a rose:
A sharp defense
Invoking sadness,
Perfecting beauty.

As Einstein proved,
The universe
Moves to chaos.
It is for us
To defy the
Laws of physics.

53

One day it
Did arrive –
What we knew,
A knock on
The door we
Did not miss.

54
―

The world too fast
To acknowledge
Your perfection,
I take it then
Upon myself.

Advice
To me:
Get rest,
And wear
The weight
Of self
Lightly.

The square refuses to square.
Geometry won't add up.
Logic has surrendered and
The puzzle has rejiggered
Its ultimate solution.

57
———

I am lost in
Patisserie's
Glass case of sweets.
Bonbon ganache,
Napoleon flats,
Raspberry whip?
Oh, the joys of
Sour postponed.

As a boy, shadows
From headlights played
Menacing games I
Watched on my ceiling.
Strange sounds heard
From the floors below.
Unable to sleep,
Stuck until dawn with
No one to hear me.

Sadness is a muse,
Replete with substance,
Craving attention.
Happiness is pure,
Ample with itself,
Free of any weight.

I leave the house behind,
And in the lower garden
I come across a rose.
Perfect in its glory,
I am aware I hold
A calling card from God.

61
―――

Today was jagged edges,
Paper cuts, loose ends
Awkward details and
Pieces that wouldn't fit.
And then we touched.

I have been too far
From shore with calls of
Help unanswered.
I talked with angels,
Felt the end, but no,
Still here, unknowing.

63

In the black pit
Of night I walk
Amongst demons
Disguised as ones
I know and trust.

64

The river of life
Flows towards happiness.
Why are we such fools
To not board a boat?

I'm a mouse
In a maze
Unaware
There is a
Scientist
Over me
With answers.

I ride my bike over cobblestones
To the promontory called Resolute.
I face west to collect some clouds.
I remember to make a wish.

After attempting a poem,
I put down my pencil as if
It was an exam completed.
I wonder were my answers right?
I will wait for the professor.

The squall left the street
Mirroring neon colors.
Traffic was slow as pedestrians
Emerged from offices
With visions of family
And early evening plans.
I picked up speed,
The city released its grip,
Buildings got smaller,
And I took one last look
In my rearview mirror.

We three, as one, emerge
From winter to first warmth,
Sunlight straining to fill
A garden coming back.
The dog smells freedom and
Runs aimlessly about,
Filled with an abandon
That we will never know.

70
———

I want to visit
My own happiness.
Explore its terrain,
Take in its brilliance,
And not be afraid.

We are artists.
The canvas is
Circumstances.
The medium:
Always kindness.

A friend's
Late marriage
Failed today.
They agreed
To let the
Puzzle be
Abandoned.

73

With age I've found
Shortcuts, methods,
Answers and more.
Wisdom, in which, rightly,
You have no interest.

We sail as one,
Barely equal
To the dangers.
I trust in us;
We will prevail.
My only fear
Is carelessness.

75

Please do not stand
Between me and
My love for you.

When we fight
Angels get
Upset and
Go *tsk, tsk*.

77
―

Cross words or
Arguments
Between us
Feels to me
Like wrong notes
Struck in a
Symphony.

Our worlds are
Splintered to,
Shards of mood,
Til our touch,
Once again,
Makes them one.

The storm is gone.
Windows rattled,
Lights flickered,
We were afraid.
Quiet again now.
Our lives returned,
Our love, intact.

Thorns on a rose,
A sharp defense
Invoking sadness,
Perfecting beauty.

81

I must
Learn to love
The child of
What I want
And what has
Happened.

I will be raised up
Not by the answer,
But by the question
Of how to love you.

83
———

Years together
And we are now
What we once hid.

I imagine
You seeing me
And how it is
Different from
You seeing me.

There is
"I love you"
And then
There is
I love you.

What do I want
To say when I
Say "I love you"?

87
―

Maybe it is
Who has loved us,
While yet never
Knowing the truth.

We live in the unknowable,
Jazz musicians improvising,
Somewhere within the mystery,
Finding notes more sweet than wishes.

Over the years
We have become
Less angular,
Smoother, like rocks
In a river,
Aligned to time.

We are in a boat
Twenty years from shore.
Beginnings are gone.
The voyage sustains.
Each day seas shift and
Yet the horizon
Is immutable.

We are dancing in the fire glow,

Experiencing the uncertainty
of separateness,

Holding each other like
apparitions,

Wondering what will happen
when we let go.

How can two hearts' desires
Be so incompatible?
Wake us from this darkness,
Save us from ourselves.

All of us at the dinner table
Have consented to conformity,
Sacrificial lambs to
Seamless conversation.
It is not for any one of us
To have impossible needs.
We chat about vacations,
And children and golf
And let our minds wander
To what it would be like to be in bed
With the one across the table.

What scares me
Is the space
Of choosing.
When all is
Available,
Who am I
To make a
Decision?

A visit to the Met.
Up stone steps,
Information rotunda,
Ancient galleries,
To a room in the back.
Alone with antiquity.
Then an intruder:
A girl with blond hair
And blue student's cap,
Admires the paintings.
Beauty both:
Art and reality.

The desire tonight
Is for something
To take
The pain
Away,
To loosen
The beast's grip,
And give a moment's
Peace.

Traffic jam afternoon
In New York City,
Hot and noisy.
I turn from Fifth Ave.
Into a red brick museum,
For the photographs of Edward Weston.
Inside it is cool.
A handful of people
Study walls of prints
From the thirties.
Portraits of his peers:
Poets and artists,
In simple settings.
A bygone era
Where what mattered
Were friends,
And the quality of the light.

Floating
On a yellow mat
Under the noon sun
In a pool in Pennsylvania,
A cloud passes,
An insect buzzes,
I lose track of time.
There is so much
To think about.
Instead,
I close my eyes
And marvel
At my ability to
Float.

My highest desire
Is to speak to you
Directly.
To say
"I love you."
Undiluted.
What stops me
Is the fear
That like the sun
The heart must be
Oblique.

100

At dinner tonight,
A party of friends,
I recalled a child
Awake in his bed,
Hearing the laughter of grown-ups.

101
———

I am the child
Awakened from
A nightmare.
A force overwhelming,
Lingers and upsets.
Parents asleep
In a room
Far away.
I am alone
And without
Salvation.

102
———

Lies.

Blackhearted bloodletters.

Shredding trust,

Extinguishing hope.

What is gained,

When all is lost?

103
―――

The answer is in my veins,
Pulsing through my body,
Tickling different nerves,
Flirting with awareness,
Hiding in my heart.

I dream of Nazis.
High ranking officers
Occupying French chateaus.
Military plans completed,
They critique the paintings.

It is odd,
After all this time,
To be dancing with you,
On this,
Your wedding day.
I wonder
What it is like,
This new,
Absolute intimacy
You've found,
And how it differs
From ours.

Difficult day.
Not enough of me
To go around.
But in this temporal,
Late night sanctuary,
Far above the failures
And loose ends,
Everything resolves.
Despite it all,
Peace.

107

She is here,
Sitting next to me.
I remain locked
In shyness and silence.
My destiny is this:
Cowardice and self-loathing.

The maestro,
Midthought,
Is distracted
And history's moment
Is lost.

109

It is hard
To let go
Of this day.
Demons -
Be patient,
I'll be yours
Soon enough.

From the doctor's office
Out to the midday street,
The sun's warmth reconnects me.
I am free now,
Free to go home.

It awaits,
Taunting, mocking,
Out of reach.
If only I were smarter,
More disciplined, better...
I can't get it.
I can't get the
ANSWER.

My children wait
With misplaced hope
Of fulfilling
Destiny.

Amidst swirling
Confusion
Comes a fragment
So brilliant
It overwhelms
Even sorrow.

I cannot sleep.
The light is on
To write these words:
Demons speak.

My goal
Is to disappear
Into the space
Between you
And truth.

He was someone who,
With his home ablaze,
Could still admire
The beauty
Of the fire.

117

Not just quiet
But a divine
Stillness,
As if the air
Had been replaced
With ether,
Pure and unstable,
Like a moment
Of love.

118

My wish is
For insight
Within the frame
Of the glorious
Common.

The Orient Express
From the mountain tunnel
Emerges at full throttle
To a winter's landscape.
From my window,
The future glistens.

Ideas carom
Like molecules.
Grab one.
Inside:
A universe.

As sleep
Incapacitates,
Dreams perch,
Waiting.

Church bells mark
The higher order:
That not forgotten
Has been forgiven.

Sleep -
An elevator ride
Past my floor
To an attic
Of imposters.

An event
Approaches,
Gathering
Darkness.
Instinct knows.

Through the tower window
Of the ancestral castle
The gimlet moon
Shimmers silver
On the highland loch.
Alone with wakefulness,
I am part of history.

A joke,
Vaudeville corny,
Against which
You are set.
Punch line,
A crinkle
Uncontrollable,
Giving way
Fully,
To laughter,
The moment
Of being seen.

Nightflight,
Like sleep,
Control surrendered.
Tranquility.
Turbulence.
Ending
With a bump
To earth.
The new day.

Art, Sensuality,
Meditation:
Ways to touch
The divine.

Enveloped by
A bittersweet sense
Of completion,
I enter the park.
Sunset colors
On lingering clouds,
Never like this.

130

Minds roiled
Hearts broken
Anguish.
And yet,
When done,
To the world
We are
Welcomed,
Anew.

Nights alone
I explore
The giddiness
Of freedom.
Untethered,
I go too far.

My heart is filled.
I want to tell you.
I can't find words.
I talk about the day.

133
———

At sunset
Of the fourth day,
I let go of earth
To join the sky
And hear the quiet
Of embracing clouds.

Angry spirits
Deep in the night
Wake me in transit:
Yesterday gone,
Not yet tomorrow.

One switch
In my brain
Left undone
Waiting
To throw
My train
Of thought
Into mayhem.

When I was young
I wanted to know why.
Now I know why,
But I tire easily.

The alchemy
Of a self-conscious
Present
Will make time
Stop.

My father pursued
Our genealogy
With a fervor
I didn't understand
Until one morning,
When I ate my cereal
Exactly as he would have.

Yes, pleasure
Is earned and
Pain appears.
Still this truth:
Each breath to
Be divine.

If there is unhappiness,
It is from being stubborn,
Gripping brokenness
Too tightly,
Not allowing rescue
By the perfect whole.

Beware the
Leeching fields
That poison
And erode.
Rise above,
And we
Will build
A castle.

Buffeted by the night
Through violent seas,
I have arrived
At harbor's light.

143

My mind is knotted,
Unable to let go.
I am stuck
With wrong ideas,
And time is
Running out.

144

The far edge
Of comfort –
Love's arena.
Overcome fear.
Find purity.

Approaching
Manhattan,
A sign for
Utopia Parkway;
I pass it by,
Believing
It will be
A disappointment.

Being unhappy
Is seeing
The road
And missing
The panorama.

Tonight,
I ignored
Voices of reason
To experience
Uncertainty,
The perilous.
I have returned
Awakened.

The hallway
Outside my bedroom,
With the pall
Of 4am stillness,
Is sinister.
The familiar
Turned frightening,
Like a lover
Strangely withdrawn.

Returning from dinner
To our small hotel,
Not ready for bed.
We pass through the bar,
Empty of patrons,
And agree
To a drink
In the garden.
Beyond the cypress trees,
The Mediterranean glistens.
The air is soft.
We chat easily
About plans
And silly
Observations.
Leaving,
We ask the bartender
To take our picture.
Before sleep,
I think of the photo
And how I will use it
In the future
To study happiness.

I am looking
For the lost
Moment
Between this
And next.

It was a room
Happened upon
In travel.
Inside,
Separated
From life
And comforted
By angels,
All was well.
I stayed
Until
I found
The reason
To leave.

Happiness stumbles,
Cruelty flashes,
Anger escalates.
From hidden sources
An unknown strength,
Intangible, elusive
Our savior,
Forgiveness.

Ah, patience –
Whispered
Request
For change,
Sweet child
Of acceptance.

I am awakened
By the racquet
Of pots and pans
Clattering to the floor.
"Are you all right?"
Your answer:
Silence.

155

The poet's
Obituary
Ends in italics:
A stanza
Of early
Divinity.

Entering the day
Anxiety awakens.
The bullets of dreams
Have now become real.

War monuments
Are carved from stone
For permanence,
The opposite
Of bravery.

Romance is
A puzzle
Never solved;
Answers stay
In our
Unconscious.

159

Let us not succumb
To the conspiracies
That would take from us
Exquisiteness.

Somewhere,
Beneath trying,
Before thinking,
Beyond wishing,
I found you.

Sacrifice
Is love's
Engine,
And we are
Mechanics,
Tinkering.

And so,
We find
Ourselves
At sea,
Together.
No land
In sight.
Exhilarated.

Intimacy
Is acceptance
In the face of
Hope failing
Truth.

Personality
Is the shell
Around what
We are
To each other.

Rattles,
Doubt and
Yearning;
The journey
Behind us,
Destiny now.

Stars aligned
The end,
Inevitable.
I see now
My surrender:
Joyous.

My mind
Stumbles,
Disappoints.
The world
Rushes in.
Amidst the
Wreckage,
All that
Remains:
Your touch.

Against reason,
We still walk
The labyrinth
Holding hands.

My house
Has been looted,
Sold to the junkman,
Stripped of dignity.
Now I can learn
About love.

Sentenced to my bed
With a broken body,
I study patience
To find a loophole.

No one knows
Our marriage.
They visit
The museum
And miss the
Masterpiece.

Errands, chores,
Obligations:
We need these
As sunglasses
To love's glare.

Pencil on paper:
Such a narrow
Conduit
For the heart.

174

From this
Too specific
Place comes,
In the distance,
A vision
Of heaven.

Awareness
In layers,
Stacked up from
Specific to cosmic,
Arrayed for
Us to choose.

Near home,
The sun
Came out.
Your arm
Through mine
You laughed,
"Over now,
Winter."

Life is filled with
Circumstances,
On top of which
Lie love, and you.

Love is
Reflection,
Moon glow.
For we can't
Embrace
The sun.

I work to tame worldly demands.
They pull at my sleeve like children,
Relentless and undisciplined.
I will not let them distract me
From you, of all, who matters most.

We are not
Romeo/Juliet.
Ah but this:
Whatever happiness
We wrestle
From life's grip,
Is treasure,
Solely ours.

181
___

Marriage
Is hoping
When you say,
You are stepping
On my toes,
It will be
Heard.

The thermostat chunks on
And from the other room
The ice machine goes clunk.
Silence for a moment,
Then this sound: a burglar?
The house is acting up
In ways it never would
If only you were here.

Polarity
Is our failure.
Let us rejoice
On common ground.

The jerry-rigged
System that is
My love for you
Is stronger than
Any happily
Ever after.

I breathe you in
To dissipate
My doubts and fear.
Comforted now,
I know I am
Where I should be.

At the end,
I will be
Satisfied,
Requesting
Only a
Kiss from you.

Meditation:
I concentrate
To dissolve my
Concentration
And find again
The great nothing.

I believe
In a realm
Out there.
No words.
No thoughts.
Tantalizingly close.

Angels lead us
To the full moon.
The stars arrayed,
Overwhelming,
Until your hand
Takes mine and
I am returned
To self and strength.

Years from now,
With hours short,
Today will
Come to mind.
Knowingly,
I will smile.

191

With patience,
We extract
Love from the
Rocks of the
Day to day.

Of all moments
Fate has chosen
This one for me
To be with you.

193

We grow old.
Nothing stays.
Against this
Only love.

Here,
At time's last stop
We edge the precipice.
Mystery solved:
I should have known
It would be you.

Tired now,
I concentrate
On a point
Of light.
As it dims,
I gently
Let go.

The time is here.
Bring down the sky.
The stars will be
Our steppingstones.

197
———

I'm done trying.
Take my hand.

198

Oh, happiness!
I take delight
In everything.
The road ends here.

Slipping away,
Eyes open, eyes closed.
Orange light. Beautiful.
Breathe, yes, deep breaths.
I should be afraid
But I'm not.
Breathe, deep breaths.
Soon to be free.

200
———

I am home,
Finally,
Satisfied.

Biography

A.H. Morris was born in NYC in December of 1949. He lived there until he married for the first time in 2006. He and his wife, Melissa, moved to New Canaan, CT where they continue to live.

His first book of poetry, *Secrets of the Universe*, was published in the fall of 2000.

His daily meditations are the source of inspiration for these poems.

He can be contacted at ahmorris200@gmail.com.

www.ingramcontent.com/pod-product-compliance
Lightning Source LLC
Chambersburg PA
CBHW051342040426
42453CB00007B/374